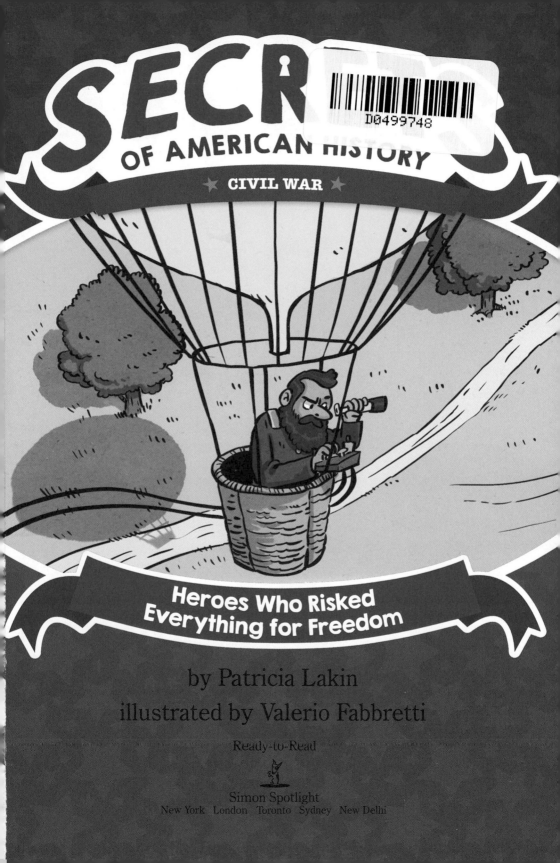

SECRETS OF AMERICAN HISTORY

★ CIVIL WAR ★

Heroes Who Risked Everything for Freedom

by Patricia Lakin

illustrated by Valerio Fabbretti

Ready-to-Read

Simon Spotlight
New York   London   Toronto   Sydney   New Delhi

SIMON SPOTLIGHT
An imprint of Simon & Schuster Children's Publishing Division
1230 Avenue of the Americas, New York, New York 10020
This Simon Spotlight edition October 2017
Text copyright © 2017 by Simon & Schuster, Inc.
Illustrations copyright © 2017 by Valerio Fabbretti

SIMON SPOTLIGHT, READY-TO-READ, and colophon are registered trademarks of Simon & Schuster, Inc.
For information about special discounts for bulk purchases, please contact Simon & Schuster Special Sales at
1-866-506-1949 or business@simonandschuster.com.
Manufactured in the United States of America 0917 LAK
2 4 6 8 10 9 7 5 3 1
Library of Congress Control Number 2017950661
ISBN 978-1-4814-9973-6 (hc)
ISBN 978-1-4814-9972-9 (pbk)
ISBN 978-1-4814-9974-3 (eBook)

Contents

Chapter I
Spies in the Civil War

What do you know about the Civil War? You might know that it took place a long time ago in America, that it was a war between the Southern and Northern states, or that it was fought over slavery.

Did you know that *spies* helped the North win the war, or that some of the bravest spies were black men and women who joined the fight for freedom after escaping slavery in the South?

Harriet Tubman was one of those spies! After she escaped slavery and led hundreds of people to freedom on the Underground Railroad (more on that later), she was a spy during the Civil War!

A man named Robert Smalls became a spy after he secretly learned hand signals used by ship captains . . . and then used them to take over a Southern ship and sail to freedom.

Learn about the stories of these inspiring heroes and many others—and about how Civil War spies used things like hot-air balloons and hollowed-out vegetables— in this book that unlocks the secrets of American history!

Before the Civil War began, there were thirty-four states. The Northern and Southern states were divided by the Mason-Dixon Line, which was named after the people who originally established it as the border between Maryland and Pennsylvania. That line was extended to form the boundary between the North and the South.

At that time, in Northern states, many people earned money by making things in factories, and slavery had been banned in most states.

In Southern states, many people earned money by owning large plantations, or farms, and slavery was legal.

Many people did the unthinkable: they bought black men, women, and children and enslaved them. These black people's rights to freedom had been taken away, and they were forced to work without pay.

In 1861, Abraham Lincoln became the sixteenth president. Some Southern states didn't want Lincoln to be president because he and his Republican Party were against slavery. They decided to leave the United States, or the Union, to form their own country called the Confederate States of America, or the Confederacy,

with Jefferson Davis as their president.
In April 1861, the Civil War began when
the Confederate army attacked the Union
army's Fort Sumter in South Carolina.

To have any chance of winning the war,
both sides needed to find out information
about their enemy. That's where spies came
in. Spies use all kinds of creative tactics
to gather information and send secret
messages, from disguises that hide a spy's
true identity to secret codes that help keep
information out of enemy hands.

Believe it or not, both sides spied on each other from the *air*, even though airplanes hadn't been invented yet. They used hot-air balloons! From inside the basket, spies could see for miles around. When they saw something important, like the size of the enemy's troops or where those soldiers were headed, they had to quickly send that information to people on the battlefield.

In those days, spies couldn't just make a phone call. Telephones hadn't been invented yet! Instead, they sometimes waved signal flags to send a message, or brought a telegraph machine on board and tapped out messages in Morse code, which were sent over telegraph wires. Morse code replaces each letter of the alphabet with dots and dashes, or quick taps and longer taps.

They also sent messages by writing them on paper and delivering them by hand. To conceal a message's meaning, they sometimes used a cipher (SY-fer). A cipher is a secret rule, device, or system that is used to mix up the letters of the alphabet. The message is then written using the mixed-up letters. Only people who know how the cipher works can decode, or translate, the message.

Ciphers were often very complicated. If the Confederates found a message written in a Union cipher and couldn't break it, or figure it out, they published the "unbreakable" message in Southern newspapers and asked readers to help decode it. Sometimes it worked, and sometimes it didn't.

Chapter 2
Harriet Tubman Was a Spy

One of the bravest spies for the Union was Harriet Tubman. She was born into slavery but escaped on the Underground Railroad. The Underground Railroad wasn't actually located underground, and it wasn't actually a railroad. It was the code name for an escape route to the Northern states, where enslaved men, women, and children could be free.

It was run by a network of people who risked their lives to provide travelers with food, shelter, and safe hiding places because they wanted to abolish, or get rid of, slavery. To keep the railroad's true purpose a secret, they used railroad terms as code words. The word "station" was used for a safe home where people could hide. The word "conductor" was used for a person who would guide enslaved people on their journey to freedom.

Tubman became a famous conductor. After escaping to the North, she used money she earned as a cook to pay her way back to the South so she could help others escape slavery through the Underground Railroad. Late at night, she would sneak onto a plantation and offer to lead any willing people North.

From 1850 to 1860, Tubman guided more than seventy people to freedom.

As a conductor Tubman used disguises to keep her identity a secret, dressing like a man or an old woman.

She also sent secret warning signals to let the people in her party know they were in danger. She mimicked the sound of an owl!

Soon Tubman's skills as a conductor were well known, but after the Civil War broke out, people stopped using the Underground Railroad, perhaps because the routes were blocked by Confederate soldiers. Tubman was asked to join President Lincoln's top secret spy ring.

She also became what was called a "scout." In 1863, Tubman led Union soldiers on a mission on South Carolina's Combahee River.

Through the spy ring, Tubman had learned that the enemy had planted torpedoes along the shore of the river. She guided the Union gunboats safely up the river, where they burned down plantation buildings, allowing about 750 people to escape slavery and sail to freedom on the Union gunboats. Many of those people went on to join the Union army and fight against their former owners in the South.

Tubman was the first woman in the history of the United States to lead an armed military attack.

Chapter 3
Secrets, Disguises, and Signals!

Spies for the Union used all kinds of tactics to get information about the Confederacy. We don't alwhays know the full names of those who had been enslaved, or in some cases even their first names. Even so, they played important roles in helping the Union win the war.

Mary Touvestre

Mary Touvestre was freed from slavery before the war began, and she became a spy for the Union. As a free woman, she found work in the home of a Confederate engineer whose job was to fix a broken-down ship called the USS *Merrimack*, or the United States Ship *Merrimack*.

Touvestre overheard the engineer talking about plans to turn the *Merrimack* into an ironclad warship, the CSS *Virginia*, or the

Confederate States Ship *Virginia*. As an "ironclad" ship it would have metal sides to protect it from the Union's attacks. Touvestre knew she had to act fast and warn the Union navy! She stole a copy of the plans and fled the Confederacy.

She crossed the border into the Union and marched straight to the office of the secretary of the navy in Washington, DC. The secretary recognized that she had very valuable information and sped up the Union's plans to complete their first ironclad warship, the USS *Monitor*, to stay one step ahead of the Confederacy.

Mary Elizabeth Bowser

Another spy, named Mary Elizabeth Bowser, had been enslaved in Virginia but was freed by her owner, Elizabeth van Lew. Van Lew didn't believe in slavery, so she helped Bowser go to school in the North to learn to read and write.

When the war began, Van Lew formed a spy ring in the South to help the Union and asked Bowser to be a spy.

According to their plan, Bowser returned from school and pretended to still be enslaved and unable to read or write since enslaved people were forbidden to do so. Van Lew helped Bowser find work in the most dangerous place for an enslaved person, which was also the best place for a spy—the Confederate White House.

While Mary served meals and cleaned, President Davis talked freely of his battle plans. He had no idea that Bowser was listening!

While she dusted his desk, she also read his important papers. Some people said she had a photographic memory and could repeat what she read word for word! Then she would pass information to Van Lew and others without being discovered as a spy.

Bowser would wait until a local baker, who was also a Union spy, made a delivery. Then she rushed outside and quietly told him information while he delivered freshly baked bread.

Bowser also gave information directly to Van Lew. They would meet at night at the edge of the Van Lew farm. After writing down what Bowser told her, Van Lew stuffed her notes inside hollowed-out eggs, and possibly even vegetables like squash, so no one would find them unless they knew where to look. Then she gave the eggs and vegetables, and the information inside them, to her contacts in the Union!

Dabney and His Wife

After fleeing to Union territory to escape slavery, a married couple became spies! The husband, Dabney, worked as a cook in a Union army camp near Fredericksburg, Virginia. His wife, whose first name is unknown, quickly left to work nearby at a home by the Confederate camp.

Soon Dabney knew all about the

Confederate troops' movements and plans before they happened. He shared the information with the Union army general, who wanted to know how Dabney had such accurate information even though he never left the Union camp.

Dabney explained that whenever his wife overheard secrets in the Confederate camp, she rushed to hang laundry on the clothesline outside the home of the woman she worked for, which he could see from the Union camp.

By hanging laundry on the line in a specific way, his wife sent different signals. A pair of pants hung upside down meant someone was traveling west, for example, and a red shirt meant it was a Confederate general called Stonewall Jackson. Two blankets pinned together at the bottom meant someone was setting a trap for Union troops!

Chapter 4
From Slavery to Freedom
on a Confederate Ship

Another future spy for the Union was Robert Smalls. He was born into slavery in 1839 in Beaufort, South Carolina, but was determined to escape.

In Beaufort, which was surrounded by water, people used boats to travel, much like we use cars today, and Smalls was a very knowledgeable boatman.

When the Civil War broke out, Smalls was hired out to work on a Confederate warship called the CSS *Planter*, which was based in Charleston, South Carolina. While Smalls worked on that ship, he hatched a risky plan. He studied how the captain walked on deck, how the captain wore his straw hat, and how the captain used hand signals. Then Smalls waited for the right moment.

On the night of May 12, 1862, the
CSS *Planter* was docked while the captain
and white crew members went on shore
for the evening. Smalls told the enslaved
men on the crew that he planned to escape
to freedom on the ship. Two men left
because they thought his plan was too
dangerous.

Smalls placed the captain's straw hat on his head and steered the ship out of the harbor. He stopped at a wharf and brought his family and other enslaved people on board.

Then Smalls, still pretending to be the captain under cover of darkness, had to pass several Confederate checkpoints without getting caught. Could he fool the Confederates into thinking he was the captain of the ship?

Smalls had studied well! He used the correct hand signals and made it past all four checkpoints. As the ship headed toward the Union blockade, Smalls pulled down the Confederate flag and replaced it with a white sheet as a sign of surrender. Smalls told the Union officers that he was giving them the ship along with its cargo of valuable weapons. He also shared information that helped the Union gain control of the Charleston harbor. Smalls had bravely guided himself and seventeen people, including his wife and children, to freedom.

Smalls was greeted as a hero in the Union and even met President Lincoln, helping to persuade him to allow black soldiers to join the Union army. Smalls eventually signed up five thousand black volunteer soldiers himself, and then joined the Union navy, became the pilot of the USS *Planter*, which was now a Union ship, and led many successful battles. For his bravery, he was promoted to the rank of brigadier general. After the war he was elected to the US House of Representatives, and he served for twelve years as a congressman for South Carolina, the same state where he had been born into slavery.

While Smalls was fighting against slavery, President Lincoln was also working to end it. In January 1863, Lincoln issued an important document called the Emancipation Proclamation. It freed, or emancipated, enslaved people who lived in states that had seceded from, or left, the Union. While it didn't end slavery in all states, it was a step toward freedom for all.

Then the Confederate president, Jefferson Davis, was captured on May 10, 1865, and the Civil War officially ended on June 2, 1865. The North and the South became the United States of America again!

The Union's path to victory was greatly helped by the bravery of countless spies and soldiers who risked their lives for justice and freedom, and their legacy lives on to this day.

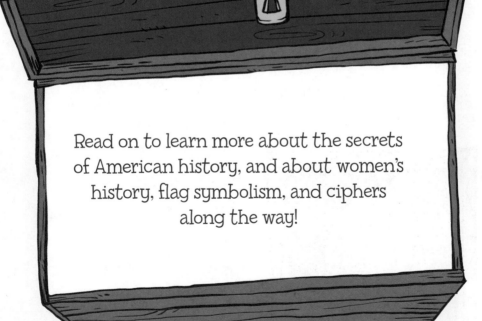

Read on to learn more about the secrets of American history, and about women's history, flag symbolism, and ciphers along the way!

Women Fought in the Civil War

Harriet Tubman wasn't the only woman on the battlefield in the Civil War. Many years before women were allowed to join the US military, women dressed as men so they could become soldiers. In the Civil War alone, it is estimated that almost four hundred women fought on the Union and Confederate sides.

Sarah Edmonds

Edmonds signed up to be a nurse in the Union army using a man's name, Franklin Thompson, possibly because she wanted an adventure. Then, when one of her friends was killed by the Confederates, she took his place as an army courier.

When she became sick with malaria, she refused

treatment out of fear that her secret would be discovered if she went to a hospital. Even after it was revealed that she was female, she was praised for her faithful service by the secretary of war and went on to receive a pension from the US government.

Frances Clayton

When Clayton's husband became a Union soldier, she pretended to be a man so she could be with him. When he was killed, she confessed that she was really a woman. She had already been wounded in battle and had survived being taken prisoner by the Confederates.

Those are just a couple of stories of women who fought in the Civil War. Others fought for a practical reason: soldiers earned much more money per month than women could earn in other kinds of jobs at that time. These brave women paved the way for the rights of future generations of women.

Stars, Stripes, and Symbols

The first official flag of the United States was adopted during the American Revolution, with the passage of the Flag Act in June 1777.

This act said that the flag should be made of "thirteen stripes, alternate red and white" and "thirteen stars, white in a blue field, representing a new Constellation."

The American flag is full of many layers of meaning, starting with the colors:

> **Red:** Stands for "hardiness and valor."
> **White:** Stands for "purity and innocence."
> **Blue:** Stands for "vigilance, perseverance, and justice."

The shapes and patterns on the flag have meanings too. At first there was a star and a stripe for each of the thirteen colonies, and a new star and stripe were added when a new state joined the Union.

So Many Stripes

Only one flag ever had more than thirteen stripes: the 1795 flag, which had fifteen stars and stripes to represent Vermont and Kentucky becoming states. In 1818 it was decided that the flag would always have thirteen stripes to represent the original colonies. More stripes made it look too crowded!

A Pattern of Stars

At first there wasn't an official pattern for the stars: stars were arranged in a circle, in rows, in the shape of a larger star, and more; and the stars often tilted in different directions!

Eventually a standard was created: fifty stars, each pointing upward, arranged in nine staggered rows and eleven staggered columns.

If you designed a flag for your home, school or family, what colors and symbols would you use? Give it a try!

Decode a Secret Message!

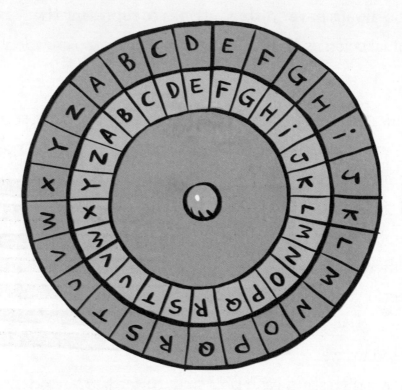

Ciphers, like the one above, were used to scramble messages during the Civil War to make them difficult to read even if they were found by the enemy.

A simple cipher pattern is to replace each letter in the alphabet with the letter that comes right after it. For example, you could replace A with B, and B with C, and so on.

Using that cipher, if you wanted to write the word "DOG," instead of writing the letter D you would write E, and so on. D-O-G would be written as E-P-H.